BERNARD STERN

VICTORIA
VERA
ZOE
GINO
MARY
TATUM
GEORGE
JOAN
JOE
JUNE
WILLIAM
TERESA
KIM
PENNY
PENELOPE
PAULINE
BEN
ANGELA
BOB
DOLLY
LILY
DORIS
BEN
ADA
MARTHA
EVE
AVRIL
SIMON
TIM
THEO
RACHEL
DESMOND
HOPE
DEAN
RAM
CLIVE
PHILLYS
BETTY
JEAN
ERROL
ENA
PHIL

BERNARD STERN

Texts by/*Textes de*/Texte von
Jean Antoine & Bernard Stern

ACADEMY EDITIONS · LONDON

ACKNOWLEDGEMENTS
Our thanks go to Bernard Stern and to
Leinster Fine Art for making material available for publication, to Holger Braasch,
Ruth Eaton, Karen Roux and Victoria
Wilson for translations, and to Prudence
Cuming Associates Limited, London,
Nathan Rabin, New York and Alain LeKim,
Paris for photography.

FRONTISPIECE
[84] *Self-Portraits* 1978

TITLE PAGE
[82] *The Leader* 1979

First published in Great Britain in 1981 by
Academy Editions 7/8 Holland Street   London W8

Printed and bound in Great Britain by
Balding + Mansell Limited, Wisbech

JEAN ANTOINE
The Power of Words/*Le pouvoir des mots*/Die Macht der Worte

My memory often functions like my camera: image-image. But it records things which will never be "framed". And it is that film – never turned into a movie – which is closest to my heart.

The event occurred in 1973. I was filming a housewarming party which Bernard Stern was holding at Carlton Hill. A man who likes architectural challenges, Bernard had bought himself a church which he had turned, quite simply, into his home and studio. That evening, buzzing around a spiral staircase which seemed to extend up to the sky, were a swarm of pretty girls, London's artistic set, a battery of projectors and . . . my cameras. In the immaculate white nave where, not long before, the acidulous strains of an organ must have wafted up, the din was resounding in decibels directly proportionate to the lowering of the levels in the champagne flutes. I had the impression that there, above the heads, was not a flight of "putti" with chubby buttocks but rather a collision of speech balloons crammed with words. And I noticed that, amidst this racket, one man remained silent: Bernard Stern. He was listening, with his customary politeness, but I am sure that he heard nothing. Nothing but the patter of words which beat against him like torrential rain beating down on a defeated Samurai in a Japanese film.

Was it on that day that Bernard Stern, unlike Nabokov who abandoned words in order to chase butterflies, decided to use his paintbrush and colours – as one would use a butterfly net – to imprison words in his pictorial vision? I don't know. But the more I think about it, the more clearly I see him, in his white suit, in the midst of these babbling and gossiping women, haloed by an enor-

Ma mémoire fonctionne souvent comme ma caméra: image-image. Mais elle enregistre ce qui ne sera jamais "cadré". Et c'est ce film-là – qui ne s'imprime sur aucune pellicule – qui me tient toujours le plus à cœur.

L'action se passait en 1973. Je filmais une "crémaillère": celle que Bernard Stern pendait à Carlton Hill. Hommes des défis architecturaux, Bernard s'était acheté une église et en avait fait, tout simplement, sa demeure et son atelier. Il y avait là, virevoltant autour d'un escalier en colimaçon qui semblait monter au ciel, un essaim de jolies filles, le "Tout-Londres-artistique", une nuée de projecteurs et . . . mes caméras. Dans la nef d'un blanc immaculé où avaient dû s'élever, peu de temps auparavant, les accents acidulés de l'harmonium, la rumeur croissait en décibels à mesure que s'abaissait le niveau des flûtes à champagne. J'avais l'impression qu'il y avait, au-dessus des têtes, non pas un envol de "putti" aux fesses pulpeuses mais un entrechoquement de phylactères gorgés de mots. Et je m'aperçus que, seul dans ce tumulte, un homme restait silencieux: Bernard Stern. Il écoutait, avec sa gentillesse coutumière, mais je suis sûr qu'il n'entendait rien. Rien d'autre que le crépitement des mots qui s'abattaient sur lui comme la pluie torrentielle peut s'abattre, dans un film japonais, sur un samouraï paumé.

A l'inverse de Nabokov qui abandonnait les mots pour chasser les papillons, est-ce ce jour-là que Bernard Stern décida d'utiliser son pinceau et ses couleurs – comme on utiliserait un filet – pour engluer les mots dans sa matière picturale? Je l'ignore. Mais plus j'y songe, plus je le vois, dans son costume blanc, au milieu de ces femmes clabaudantes et papotantes, nimbé d'une énorme bulle étrangement vierge!

Je me souviens aussi, bien sûr, de ce portrait du prolétaire-culturel, Michael Kustow, une très grande toile qui occupait, dans cette église, la place

Mein Gedächtnis funktioniert oft wie meine Kamera: Bild-Bild-Bild, aber es hält Dinge fest, die man niemals »rahmen« kann, und gerade dieser Film – der nie ein »abendfüllender« Film sein wird – liegt mir am meisten am Herzen.

Es geschah 1973. Ich filmte eine Einweihungsparty, die Bernard Stern in seiner Wohnung am Carlton Hill gab. Bernard liebt die architektonische Herausforderung. Er hatte sich eine Kirche gekauft und diese einfach zu einer Wohnung und einem Atelier umgebaut. An jenem Abend schwärmte es von schönen Mädchen und Eingeweihten der Londoner Kunstszene, die sich um eine Wendeltreppe scharten, welche bis in den Himmel zu reichen schien. Es summten eine ganze Batterie von Projektoren und . . . meine Kameras. In einem Kirchenschiff von absolut reinem Weiß, durch das vor noch nicht langer Zeit die säuerlichen Melodien der Orgel schwebten, hallte der Lärm in einer Dezibelstärke proportional zum sinkenden Pegel in den Sektgläsern wider. Es kam mir vor, als ob über unseren Köpfen nicht Putten mit drallen Hinterbacken umherflogen, sondern mit Wörtern überladene Sprechblasen zusammenstießen. Ich bemerkte auch, daß ein Mann inmitten dieses Tumultes stumm blieb, nämlich Bernard Stern. Er lauschte in seiner ihm eigenen sanften Art, doch hörte er bestimmt nichts. Nichts außer einem tösenden Schwall von Worten, der auf ihn niederprasselte, ähnlich dem Wolkenbruch in einem japanischen Film, der auf einen besiegten Samurai niederprasselt.

Hat Bernard Stern sich wohl an diesem Tag entschieden – anders als Nabokov, der die Worte hinter sich ließ, um Schmetterlinge zu fangen – Pinsel und Farbe dazu zu benutzen, Worte in seiner malerischen

[83] *Golden Idol* 1979

mous, strangely blank speech balloon.

I also remember, of course, a portrait of the cultural proletarian Michael Kustow – a very large canvas which occupied, in this church, the position which might have been taken by an "Assumption". As an intellectual porter in a market, Kustow stood out against a superb background of graffiti. The picture reeked of Covent Garden. There was, in fact, on the same wall, a magical still life: crates of fruit. These crates of fruit are one of the keys to Stern's universe. He knows the weight of these crates, because he carried them, during the sombre hours of the war, in a Covent Garden which was, at that time, nothing like the fashionable district it is today. A Jonas, toiling and penniless, Bernard was plunged into the "bowels" of London. But from this descent into hell, into the debauchery of fruit and vegetables where he had toiled, he was to retain an acute sense of fresh and subtle colours and – perhaps unconsciously, for some later time – a very keen awareness of the language of walls.

For each great painter there is a moment of trial in which he stores up, without realizing it, the material which will ultimately allow him to arrive at his own manner, his own style. A moment of confusion in which he has

qu'aurait pu prendre une "Assomption": en fort des Halles intellectuel, Kustow se détachait sur un superbe fond de graffiti. Cela sentait son "Covent Garden" à plein nez. Il y avait, d'ailleurs, sur le même mur, une nature morte féerique: des cageots de fruits. Ces cageots de fruits qui sont une des clefs de l'univers de Stern. Il en connaît le poids de ces cageots, car il les a portés, aux sombres heures de la guerre, dans ce Covent Garden qui n'avait rien, alors, du quartier à la mode qu'il est aujourd'hui. Jonas ahanant et sans le sous, Bernard était plongé dans le "ventre" de Londres. Mais de cette descente aux enfers, dans la débauche de fruits et légumes où il avait peiné, il conserverait un sens aigu des couleurs fraîches et subtiles, et – peut-être inconsciemment, pour plus tard – une attention très vive aux langages des murs.

Pour chaque grand peintre il y a un moment d'épreuve où il engrange, sans le savoir, les matériaux qui lui permettront, ultérieurement, d'arriver à sa manière, à son style. Un moment de désarroi où il lui faut aller au bout de la solitude, comme pour mieux se fortifier dans ce métier où il sera toujours seul face à son chevalet. Covent Garden a été, pour Bernard Stern, ce que fut le Borinage pour Van Gogh. Je l'imagine, à la fin d'une journée épuisante, ponctuée par les alertes et les bombardements, errant dans des rues mal éclairées et pleines de poussière. Il n'a pas tellement envie de se retrouver dans l'atelier triste où l'attend

Vision einzufangen, so wie man ein Schmetterlingsnetz benutzt? Ich weiß es nicht. Je mehr ich jedoch darüber nachdenke, um so deutlicher sehe ich ihn in seinem weißen Anzug, umgeben von plappernden, klatschenden Frauen, mit einer leeren Sprechblase über seinem Kopf.

Ich erinnere mich natürlich auch an ein sehr großes Gemälde, ein Portrait des Kulturproletariers Michael Kustow, das hier in dieser Kirche an der Stelle hing, wo man vielleicht sonst eine »Himmelfahrt« erwartet hätte. Wie ein intellektueller Lastenträger auf einem Markt hob sich Kustow von dem Graffiti-Hintergrund ab. Das Bild roch geradezu nach Covent Garden. An derselben Wand hing übrigens noch ein magisches Stilleben: Kisten mit Obst gefüllt, jene Obstkisten, die zu den Schlüsseln zu Sterns Universum gehören. Er weiß, wie schwer diese Kisten sind, da er sie in düsteren Kriegsstunden im Covent Garden Markt, der damals mit dem eleganten Viertel von heute nichts gemein hatte, getragen hat. Bernard, der keinen Pfennig besaß, wurde wie ein Jonas in den »Bauch« Londons geworfen. Doch diese Höllenfahrt mit ihrer Schufterei und ihrer Übersättigung mit Obst und Gemüse sollte ihm ein scharfes Gespür für frische und subtile Farben und – später

[17] *A Writing Mirror* 1978

to go to the depths of solitude, as if to strengthen himself for this profession where he will always be alone, face to face with his easel. Covent Garden has been, for Bernard Stern, what the Borinage was for Van Gogh. I can imagine him, at the end of an exhausting day punctuated by sirens and bombings, wandering in the dark and dusty streets. He doesn't really want to go back to the sad studio where an unfinished canvas awaits him: an English boat sunk by the Luftwaffe. Everything is sinking, everything is collapsing in this period of the Blitz. Who still dares to utter the work "hope"? Then, in the semi-darkness, to the tune of a wailing siren, Bernard stops in front of a decaying wall and deciphers four huge letters written in chalk by a mad or unconscious creature: "l-o-v-e". No, he isn't mistaken, he isn't suffering from an hallucination. He has read it correctly: "love". Walls do not have ears, contrary to the claim of a stupid piece of propaganda, but they do have feelings. From that day onwards, Bernard Stern never ceased to hold an impassioned dialogue with them.

Forty years of work, the slow maturing of a craft and a technique, the almost systematic

une toile inachevée: un bateau anglais coulé par la Luftwaffe. Tout s'effondre, tout s'écroule dans cette période du Blitz. Qui oserait encore prononcer le mot "espoir"? C'est alors que Bernard, dans la pénombre et dans le hululement d'une sirène, s'arrête devant un mur lépreux et déchiffre ces quatre lettres écrites à la craie par un fou ou un inconscient: "l-o-v-e". Oui, il ne s'est pas trompé, il n'est pas en proie à une hallucination. Il a bien lu: "love". Les murs n'ont pas d'oreilles, contrairement à ce que proclame une propagande idiote, mais ils ont des sentiments. De ce jour, Bernard Stern n'arrêtera plus d'avoir, avec eux, un dialogue passionné.

Quarante ans de travail, la lente maturation d'un métier et d'une technique, l'investigation presque systématique de domaines électifs: la femme, la famille, les clowns, les présidents, les fruits, les arches et les villes, n'auront pas été de trop pour que Bernard Stern osât enfin entreprendre sa première composition sur des graffiti. Quel est le mot qu'il inscrit spontanément sur un fond aux couleurs de soufre et de sang? Le mot "love", bien sûr. Avec, en hommage à ses adeptes, beaucoup de "lovers" qui s'entrecroisent, qui se superposent, qui s'enlacent dans une guirlande de jambages. Il finira par écrire, dans an autre tableau: "they're lovesick". Et puis il s'envolera pour le Pérou.

Bernard m'a raconté que ce voyage au Pérou fut la résultante d'un geste véritablement surréaliste. Il était à New York, l'hiver se traînait – c'était en 1979 – et, lassé du vent glacial et de la pluie, il résolut d'aller à la rencontre du soleil. Mais dans quel pays? Il n'avait aucune préférence. Il étala devant lui une carte de l'Amérique Latine, prit une épingle, ferma les yeux et, dans ce mouvement qu'elle fait quotidiennement de la palette au tableau, souleva la main pour la faire retomber ausitôt et planter l'aiguille au hasard.

J'ai toujours été persuadé qu'il n'y avait pas de hasard pour les artistes. Qu'ils le veuillent ou non, ils font flèche de tout bois. Dans ce cas, la flèche s'était enfoncée sous le mot "Lima". Bernard était au Pérou le lendemain.

On pourrait dire qu'il n'a rien vu au Pérou, comme il n'entend rien dans le brouhaha des vernissages et des cocktails. Mais, dans la banlieue de Lima, les murs, une fois de plus, lui ont fait de troublantes confidences. Il est parvenu ensuite à faire réappara-

vielleicht unbewußt – eine außerordentlich wache Aufmerksamkeit für die »Sprache der Wände« geben.

Für jeden großen Maler kommt einmal die Stunde der Prüfung, wenn er, ohne es selbst zu wissen, das Material speichert, das es ihm letztendlich ermöglicht, seinen eigenen Stil zu entwickeln. Ein Augenblick der Verwirrung, in dem er bis an die äußersten Grenzen der Einsamkeit gehen muß, sozusagen um sich besser für seinen Beruf zu wappnen, in dem er dann immer mit sich allein vor seiner Staffelei stehen wird. Für Bernard Stern hat Covent Garden dieselbe Rolle gespielt wie die Borinage für Van Gogh. Ich kann mir vorstellen, wie er am Ende eines anstrengenden, von Sirenen und Bomben unterbrochenen Tages in den dunklen, staubigen Straßen umherwanderte. Er spürte kein besonderes Bedürfnis, in das traurige Zimmer zurückzukehren, in dem ihn ein noch unvollendetes Bild erwartete, ein von der Luftwaffe versenktes, englisches Schiff. Alles war im Begriff zu sinken, während des »Blitzes« in sich zusammen zu stürzen. Wer hätte es damals noch gewagt, das Wort »Hoffnung« in den Mund zu nehmen? In jenem Moment blieb er im Halbdunkel beim Klang klagender Sirenen vor einer brüchigen Wand stehen und entzifferte vier Buchstaben, die vielleicht ein Verrückter mit Kreide daraufgeschrieben hatte: »l-o-v-e«. Nein, es war kein Irrtum, er litt nicht an Halluzinationen. Er hatte richtig gelesen: »love«. Wände haben keine Ohren, aber sie haben Gefühle, im Gegensatz zu dem, was die Propaganda behauptet. Von diesem Tag an sollte Bernard Stern einen unentwegten, leidenschaftlichen Dialog mit ihnen führen.

Vierzig Jahre Arbeit, der langsamen Reifung eines Handwerks und einer Technik, der nahezu systematischen Erforschung elektiver Bereiche: die Frau, die Familie, Clowns, Präsidenten, Früchte, die Arche Noah und Städte waren wahrscheinlich keiner allzu großen Ordnung unterworfen, als daß Bernard Stern nicht schließlich den ersten Versuch einer Graffiti-Komposition gewagt hätte. Was ist das erste Wort, das er spontan auf einen schwefel- und blutfarbenen Hintergrund aufträgt? Natürlich das Wort »love«,

investigation of elective domains – woman, the family, clowns, presidents, fruit, Noah's Arks and cities – this was not too much in order for Bernard Stern to dare at last to undertake his first graffiti composition. What was the first word which he spontaneously inscribed on a blood and sulphur-coloured background? The word "love", of course. With, in homage to his followers, several "lovers" intertwined, superimposed, interlaced with one another in a sort of garland of limbs. He was to end up by writing, in another painting: "they're lovesick". And then he flew off to Peru.

Bernard has told me how this voyage to Peru was the result of a truly surrealist gesture. He was in New York, winter was dragging on – it was in 1979 – and, tired of the icy wind and the rain, he resolved to go to meet the sun. But in which country? He had no preference. He spread out in front of him a map of Latin America, took a pin, closed his eyes, and, with that movement which he makes every day from palette to painting, raised his hand and stuck in the pin at random.

I have always been sure that there is no such thing as chance for artists. Whether they like it or not, every event leads to a purpose, as yet unknown. In this case, the pin was stuck in underneath the word "Lima". Bernard was in Peru the next day.

One could say that he didn't see anything in Peru, just as he didn't hear anything amidst the hubbub of private views and cocktails. But in the outskirts of Lima, the walls once more told him their disturbing secrets. Afterwards, he succeeded in making Peru reappear in successive layers, on reams of Chinese paper bought in New York. A Peru trapped in coca like a seagull caught in a black tide. A Peru of jade and gems in which gold, a long, long time ago, had been turned into lead. A vibrant, incandescent Peru in which advertizing slogans shout to the rhythm of Inca music and where Jesus' only power of redemption is as the name of a mineral water. Bernard Stern is the painter of dazzling derision. Those words – "salud", "pueblo", "Pepsi", "Bolivar", "mejor" – whose conno-

être le Pérou, par strates successives, sur des rames de papier de Chine achetées à New York. Un Pérou empoissé de coca, comme une mouette prise dans la marée noire. Un Pérou de jade et de cabochons où l'or, depuis belle lurette, s'est transformé en un plomb vil. Un Pérou trépidant, incandescent où les slogans publicitaires s'impriment sur un rythme de musique inca et où Jésus n'a d'autre vertu rédemptrice que celle d'une eau minérale. Bernard Stern est le peintre de la dérision coruscante. Ces mots: "salud", "pueblo", "Pepsi", "Bolivar", "mejor" dont les connotations, dans les bleus intenses, les rouges-flamme ou les vert-de-gris, se répercutent à l'infini, lui ont permis – bien au-delà de ce que peuvent faire les "conceptuels" – de nous donner à voir ce qui se cachait depuis des siècles dans la mystérieuse expression française: "ce n'est pas le Pérou"!

Bernard Stern est, comme il le dit, un peintre sériel. J'irais jusqu'à le baptiser "dodécaphoniste" – bien qu'il soit plus mozartien que schönbergien – dans la mesure où, d'une palette qui a la richesse de celles d'un Ensor ou d'un Bonnard, il n'hésite jamais à utiliser toute la gamme des tons et des demi-tons. Ce que je veux dire, c'est qu'à partir d'un thème "plastique", il envisage toujours toutes les variations, inversions, récurrences, à l'instar d'un compositeur sériel. Comme s'il lui fallait épuiser le jeu des possibles. Aller jusqu'au bout de ce que son intuition et son expérience lui commandent.

Il n'y a, finalement, rien de fortuit dans ses démarches successives – qui ne sont pas des "époques" comme les historiens d'art aiment à en définir, mais de véritables partitions où toutes libertés sont laissées aux interprètes visuels que nous sommes.

Un détail, mais il a son importance. Au retour du Pérou, Bernard me montre une des premières toiles du fascinant ensemble qui fait l'objet de ce livre: ce théâtre d'ombres fugitives inscrites sur des palissades pleines de murmures. Une chose me frappe aussitôt: sur les planches qui ont repris la forme des horizons newyorkais qu'il peignait précédemment, Bernard écrit ses lettres au pochoir. Comme elles l'étaient sur les cageots de Covent Garden! Et non pas dans les tableaux de Jasper Johns, de Braque ou de Lissitzky, car Bernard Stern obéit bien davantage à ses instincts qu'à ses connaissances artistiques.

und dazu viele ineinander verschlungene, übereinanderliegende, in einer Art von Girlande von Gliedmaßen verflochtene »lovers«. Schließlich wird er in einem anderen Bild schreiben: »they're lovesick«. Und dann fliegt er nach Peru.

Bernard hat mir erzählt, wodurch sich die Reise nach Peru ergab – verursacht durch eine wahrhaft surrealistische Geste. Er war in New York, der Winter zog sich hin – das war 1979 – und des eisigen Windes und des Regens müde, entschloß er sich, die Sonne aufzusuchen. Die Frage aber war, in welchem Land? Bestimmte Vorstellungen hatte er nicht. Er breitete eine Karte Lateinamerikas vor sich aus, nahm eine Nadel, schloß die Augen und mit jener Bewegung, die er jeden Tag von der Palette zur Leinwand macht, hob er die Hand und setzte die Nadel aufs Geratewohl auf.

Ich bin schon immer der Auffassung gewesen, daß es für Künstler so etwas wie Glück nicht gibt. Jedes Ereignis hat seinen Zweck, wenn auch noch unbekannt, ob er es will oder nicht. In diesem Fall stak die Nadel unter dem Wort »Lima«. Am nächsten Tag war Bernard in Peru.

Man könnte behaupten, daß er von Peru nichts gesehen hat, genauso wenig wie er im Gewimmel der Vernissagen und Cocktailparties etwas gehört hat. Doch am Stadtrand von Lima vetrauten ihm die Wände ein weiteres Mal ihre Sorgen an. Danach gelang es ihm, auf ganzen Stößen des in New York gekauften chinesischen Papieres in vielen Schichten bemalt Peru wiedererscheinen zu lassen. Ein in Coca gefangenes Peru, gleich einer von einer schwarzen Sturmwelle erfaßten Seemöwe. Ein Peru aus Jade und Schmuck, in dem schon vor langer Zeit Gold in Blei verwandelt worden war. Ein vibrierendes, grelles Peru, wo Werbeslogans dem Rythmus der Inkamusik folgen, und wo Jesus' Rolle als Erlöser nichts weiter als der Markenname eines Mineralwassers zu seien scheint. Bernard Stern ist der Maler des brillianten Spottes. Jene Wörter – »salud«, »pueblo«, »Pepsi«, »Bolivar«, »mejor« – deren Begriffe in intensiven Blautönen, flammendem Rot oder »vert-de-gris« bis ins

[128] *Starry Night* 1980

10

[93] *Life in the Streets (Evening)* 1980

tations, in intense blues, flame-reds and "vert-de-gris", reverberate into infinity, have allowed him – well beyond anything the "conceptuals" can do – to enable us to see what has been hidden for centuries in that mysterious French expression: "ce n'est pas le Pérou".

Bernard Stern is, as he himself says, a serial painter. I would even go so far as to christen him "dodecaphonist" – even though he is more Mozartian than Schönbergian – in so far as, from a palette which has the richness of Ensor or Bonnard, he never hesitates to use the whole scale of tones and semi-tones. What I mean is that, taking a "plastic" theme as his point of departure, he always envisages all the variations, inversions and recurrences, in the manner of a serial composer. As if he needed to exhaust the possibilities, to go to the end of what his intuition and experience compel him to do.

Finally, there is nothing fortuitous in his successive steps – which are not "periods" as art historians like to define them, but rather veritable partitions where all liberties are left to the visual interpreters that we are.

A detail, but with a certain importance. On returning from Peru, Bernard showed me one of the first canvases of the fascinating collection which forms the subject of this book: a theatre of fleeting shadows inscribed on hoardings full of whispers. One thing struck me straight away: on the planks which had again taken up the form of the New York horizons of his previous paintings, he had written the letters with a stencil. As they were on the crates at Covent Garden! And not as in the paintings of Jasper Johns, Braque or Lissitzky, because Bernard follows his instinct rather than his knowledge of art.

This provided the impetus. From the relatively subordinate role which it had had before, graffiti moved to the foreground. And the stencil gave it the nobility of lapidary inscriptions. It was soon, in its accumulation, to find the impulsiveness of a verbal tide and the stridency of cries.

It would need the combined efforts of an

[126] Study for *Easy Rider* 1980

[131] *Concerto* 1981

Unendliche widerhallen, haben es ihm ermöglicht – und zwar weit über die Grenzen der »Konzeptionisten« hinaus – uns sehen zu machen, was jahrhundertelang in dem geheimnisvollen französischen Ausdruck »ce n'est pas le Pérou« verborgen lag.

Bernard Stern ist (auch gemäß eigener Aussage) ein Serienmaler. Ich würde sogar soweit gehen, ihn einen »Dodekaphonisten« zu nennen, obwohl er eher Mozart als Schönberg zuzurechnen ist, schon dadurch, daß er nie zögert, die gesamte Skala von Tönen und Halbtönen einer Palette zu benutzen, deren Vielfalt den Paletten eines Ensor oder eines Bonnards entspricht. Was ich damit sagen möchte, ist, daß er sich ein »plastisches« Thema als Ausgangspunkt wählt und dabei alle Variationen, Inversionen, Wiederholungen nach der Art eines Serienkomponisten im Auge hat, als ob er den Weg bis zu Ende gehen müßte, der ihm von seiner Eingebung und Erfahrung zwingendermaßen vorgezeichnet wird.

Letzten Endes bleibt in dieser Schritt-für-Schritt-Folge nichts dem Zufall überlassen. Und es sind auch keine »Epochen«, wie sie so gern von Kunsthistorikern bezeichnet werden, sondern Partituren, bei denen uns als deren visuellen Interpreten, die wir zweifellos sind, sämtliche Freiheit gelassen wird.

Noch ein wichtiges Detail. Nach seiner Rückkehr aus Peru zeigte mir Bernard das erste seiner Bilder dieser faszinierenden Gruppe, um die sich dieses Buch dreht: das Schauspiel flüchtiger Schatten auf einer von Geflüster übersäten Bretterwand. Mir fiel sofort auf, daß er die Buchstaben auf den Bretterzäunen, welche die Form des New Yorker Horizontes wiedererahnen lassen, wie schon in früheren Gemälden, mit Hilfe einer Schablone aufträgt. Genauso wie sie auf den Kisten in Covent Garden zu sehen sind! Und gar nicht so wie in den Bildern von Jasper Johns, Braque oder Lissitzky, denn Bernard folgt seinem Instinkt stärker als seinem künstlerischen Wissen.

Dieses gab den Anstoß. Das Graffiti löst sich aus der relativ untergeordneten Rolle von früher und rückt in den Vordergrund. Dabei

epigraphist, a linguist and a structuralist philosopher to analyse this logograph which has become a sort of "matière brute". Perhaps a computer which added up the words in English, French, Franglais and that vocabulary which no longer has a fatherland, could reveal to us all the obsessions and secret impulses of Bernard Stern. What does it matter?

What is new and striking is to see words literally fly away. ("Les poètes ont perdu leurs paroles" Bernard had written, almost embossed, on a watercolour which is both an alphabet and a very confidential message.) The prodigious thing is to be able to evaluate the weight of language to the measure of Hertzian waves. And to have at last before our very eyes the graphics of our senseless speed races, our resounding speeches and our future atomization on the walls of our cities.

My eye-camera has recorded – in the space of about two years – the passage of a young girl on a scooter (as important as the young girl with the hoop in the famous painting by de Chirico), of a motorcyclist bucking up his machine, of amateur and professional cyclists pursued by snarling dogs, of out-of-breath joggers, of New York phantoms rollerskating, finally of footballers taken at that point in the maelstrom of vociferations when one only catches glimpses of a thigh, socks and a ball. That's just part of the story.

But it is the bursting forth of all this into real partitions, where words, suddenly, with the complicity of violins, attack intangible staves, which brings us to a "fermata". The hoardings have given way to sheets of music. Bernard Stern arrives at the end of a symphonic movement. He is moving towards other things of which neither he nor we are yet aware, to the sound of those words whose power he would like to discover.

L'impulsion est donnée. Les graffiti, du rôle relativement accessoire qu'ils avaient auparavant, passent au premier plan. Et le pochoir leur confère la noblesse des inscriptions lapidaires. Ils trouveront bientôt, dans leur accumulation, l'impétuosité du flot verbal et la stridence des cris.

Il faudrait les efforts conjugués d'un épigrapiste, d'un linguiste et d'un philosophe structuraliste pour analyser cette logorrhée devenue une sorte de matière brute. Peut-être qu'un ordinateur qui ferait le compte des mots anglais, français, franglais et de ces vocables qui n'ont pas de patrie, nous dirait tout sur les obsessions et les pulsions secrètes de Bernard Stern. Peu importe.

Ce qui est neuf et saisissant, c'est de voir, littéralement, des paroles s'envoler ("Les poètes ont perdu leurs paroles" avait écrit Bernard, presque en filigrane, dans une aquarelle qui est à la fois un abécédaire et un message très confidentiel). Ce qui est prodigieux, c'est de pouvoir mesurer le poids du langage à l'aune des ondes hertziennes. Et d'avoir enfin, sous les yeux, le graphique de nos courses insensées, de nos discours tonitruants et de notre atomisation future sur les murs de nos cités.

Mon œil-caméra a enregistré – en l'espace de deux ans à peu près – le passage d'une petite fille en trottinette (aussi importante que la petite fille au cerceau du fameux tableau de Chirico), d'un motard cabrant sa monture, de cyclistes amateurs et professionnels poursuivis par des clébards hargneux, de joggeurs essoufflés, de fantômes newyorkais patinant à roulettes, enfin de footballeurs pris à tel point dans le tourbillon des vociférations qu'on n'apercevait plus d'eux qu'une cuisse, des jambières et un ballon. Voilà pour la petite histoire.

Mais que tout cela ait débouché sur de vraies partitions, où les mots, tout à coup, avec la complicité des violons, ont pris d'assaut les portées intangibles, voilà qui nous amène au point d'orgue. La palissade a fait place au cahier de musique. Bernard Stern arrive au terme d'un mouvement symphonique. Il glisse vers autre chose qu'il ignore, que nous ignorons, dans la résonance de ces mots dont il voulait connaître le pouvoir.

verleiht ihm der Einsatz der Schablone die Vornehmheit lapidarer Aufschriften. Bald werden sie in ihrer Gesamtheit die Wildheit verbaler Flutwellen und den grellen Ton von Schreien annehmen.

Das Neue, Frappierende ist, zu sehen, wie Wörter im wahrsten Sinne des Wortes davonfliegen. (»Les poètes ont perdu leurs paroles«, hatte Bernard auf ein Aquarell, das gleichzeitig Alphabet und vertrauliche Mitteilung darstellt, geschrieben, ja, fast eingraviert.) Das Erstaunliche ist, daß man das Gewicht der Sprache an der Frequenz der Hertzschen Wellen messen kann. Und daß wir vor unseren eigenen Augen die graphische Darstellung unserer sinnlosen Raserei, unseres überlauten Geschwätzes und unserer künftigen Auflösung in Atome auf den Wänden unserer Städte sehen können.

Mein Auge als Kamera hat im Laufe von zwei Jahren ein vorbeifahrendes kleines Mädchen auf seinem Tretroller (von gleicher Bedeutung wie das junge Mädchen mit dem Reifen in dem berühmten Bild von Chirico), einen Motorradfahrer, der seine Maschine anwirft, von knurrenden Hunden verfolgte Amateur- und Berufsradfahrer, atemlose Dauerläufer, New Yorks rollschuhlaufende Gespenster und schließlich auch Fußballspieler festgehalten, die allesamt so tief in den Strudel des umgebenden Geschreies geraten sind, daß man nur noch flüchtige Blicke auf Schenkel, Socken oder einen Ball werfen kann. Aber das ist nur ein Aspekt von vielen.

Das Faszinierende aber ist, daß sich all dieses in eine Partitur ergießt, in der die Wörter plötzlich wie in geheimer Absprache mit den Geigen unberührbare Notenlinien angreifen. Die Bretterzäune weichen den Notenblättern. Bernard Stern erreicht den Höhepunkt, das Ende eines symphonischen Satzes. Er bewegt sich nun anderen uns und ihm anbekonnten Dingen zu, zum Klange jener Wörter, deren Macht wir gerne entdecken würden.

[117] *Last Effort* 1980

14

[129] *Rehearsal* 1981 →

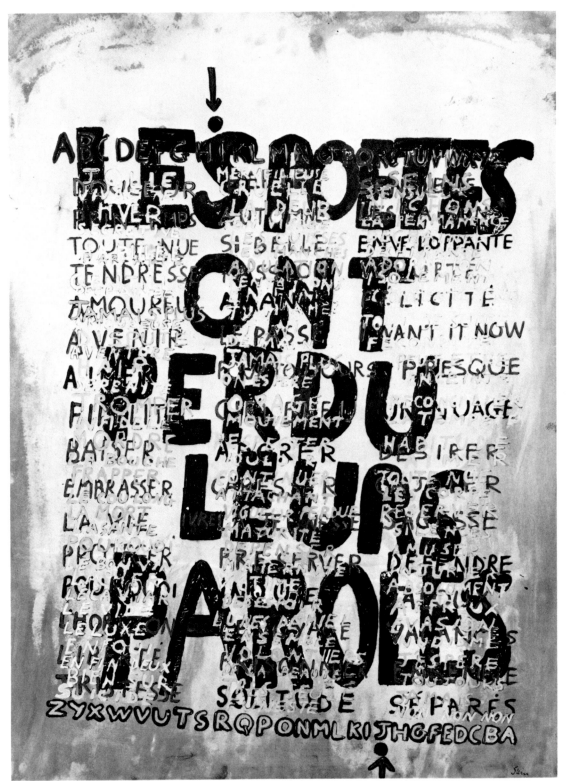

[19] *Les Poètes ont Perdu Leurs Paroles* 1978

16

BERNARD STERN
Obsessions/*Obsessions*/Obsessionen

"This power ... reveals itself in the balance or reconcilement of opposite or discordant qualities: of sameness, with difference; of the general with the concrete; the idea with the image; the individual with the representative; the sense of novelty and freshness with old and familiar objects; a more than usual state of emotion with more than usual order; judgement ever awake and steady self-possession with enthusiasm and feeling profound or vehement ..."

Samuel Taylor Coleridge on the imagination in poetic genius, from *Biographia Literaria* (1817) Vol. II, Chapter XIV

The present book covers a period of just over three years of work – and illustrates the result of a long struggle to identify my commitment to and my obsession with painting phases of human emotions. These paintings are about love, distress, loneliness, fear, power, noise, music and so on. They are about violence, too. Primarily they are about people locked in the "word curtains" of their own expression.

In his book *The Sound Structure of Music*, Robert Erickson says: "we cannot close our ears: we have no ear lids". This phrase was the concrete expression of my belief. Why not add yet another dimension in a painting, a sort of speech and noise envelope?

In paintings such as *Crowd Noise, Fans Cheering, Violence, Marathon* and others I wanted to depict the visual/aural experience. We are living *at* and *in* a time when words and images assault us from every direction. Like a surging tide, noise and words bombard us in the cities, at work and at play. Most of us live within the limits of the vocabulary of our own private world. Tele-

---

"Cette force ... se révèle dans l'équilibre ou le rapprochement de qualités opposées ou discordantes: le semblable et le différent; le général et le concret; l'idée et l'image; l'individu et le type; la notion de nouveauté et de fraîcheur, et de vieux objets familiers; un état émotif d'une intensité inhabituelle et un ordre exceptionnellement parfait; un jugement essentiellement vigilant et une bonne maîtrise de soi, opposés à un enthousiasme et un sentiment profond ou véhément ..."

De l'imagination dans le génie poètique par Samuel Taylor Coleridge, Biographia Literaria *(1817) Tome II, Chapitre XIV*

Ce livre concerne les trois dernières années de mon travail: résultat d'une longue recherche d'identifier mon engagement et mon obsession à vouloir peindre des aspects différents des émotions humaines. Mes toiles parlent d'amour, de détresse, de solitude, de peur, du pouvoir, du bruit, de la musique ... de la violence aussi ... et surtout d'êtres humains enveloppés dans leurs propres "rideaux de paroles".

Dans The Sound Structure of Music, *Robert Erickson dit: "we cannot close our ears: we have no ear lids" (Nous ne pouvons pas fermer nos oreilles). Cette phrase concrétise mes propres convictions. Pourquoi ne pas ajouter une autre dimension à la peinture, une sorte d'envelope de paroles et de bruit?*

Dans des tableaux tels que Crowd Noise, Fans Cheering, Violence, Marathon *et d'autres encore, je voulais peindre l'expérience audio-visuelle. Dans le monde où nous vivons aujourd'hui, mots et images nous assaillent de toutes parts. En ville, au travail, dans les loisirs, bruits et paroles se jettent sur nous comme une mer houleuse. Nous sommes souvent prisonniers du vocabulaire de notre univers particulier. Le langage télégraphique est à l'ordre du jour.*

»*Die Gleichgewichtigkeit oder der Ausgleich gegensätzlicher oder widersprüchlicher Eigenschaften, der Gleichheit mit Unterschiedlichkeit, des Allgemeinen mit dem Konkreten, der Idee mit dem Bild, des Individuellen mit dem Repräsentativen, des Sinnes für Neues und Erfrischendes mit alten, vertrauten Objekten, ein mehr als gewöhnlicher emotioneller Zustand mit einer mehr als üblichen Ordnung, ein ständig wachsames Beurteilungsvermögen und beständige Selbstbeherrschung verbunden mit Enthusiasmus und einem tiefen oder leidenschaftlichen Gefühl ...*«

Samuel Taylor Coleridge über die Vorstellungskraft des dichterischen Genies. Aus *Biographia Literaria* (1817) Band II, Kap. XIV

Das vorliegende Buch befaßt sich mit einer Arbeitsperiode von mehr als drei Jahren und stellt das Ergebnis eines langen Kampfes um die Identifizierung meiner Entschlossenheit und meiner Obsession dar, die Phasen menschlicher Emotionen bildlich wiederzugeben. Meine Gemälde handeln von der Liebe, von der Not, von der Einsamkeit, Ängsten, Macht, Lärm, Musik, von der Gewalt. Sie handeln in erster Linie von den Menschen, die in den »Wortvorhängen« ihrer eigenen Äußerungen verfangen sind.

Robert Erickson sagt in seinem Buch *The Sound Structures of Music:* »we cannot close our ears: we have no earlids« (Wir können unsere Ohren nicht schließen. Wir haben keine Ohrenlider). Dieser Worte waren der Inbegriff meiner Auffassang. Warum einem Gemälde nicht eine weitere Dimension verleihen, eine Art von Sprech- und Lärmrahmen?

Bei den Gemälden wie *Crowd Noise, Fans*

[1] *Landscape Through a Curtain* 1975–76

[2] *Curtain on a View* 1975–76

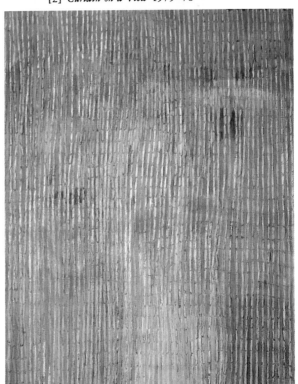

[5] *Landscape Through a Curtain I* 1976–77

[8] *Les Rideaux* 1978

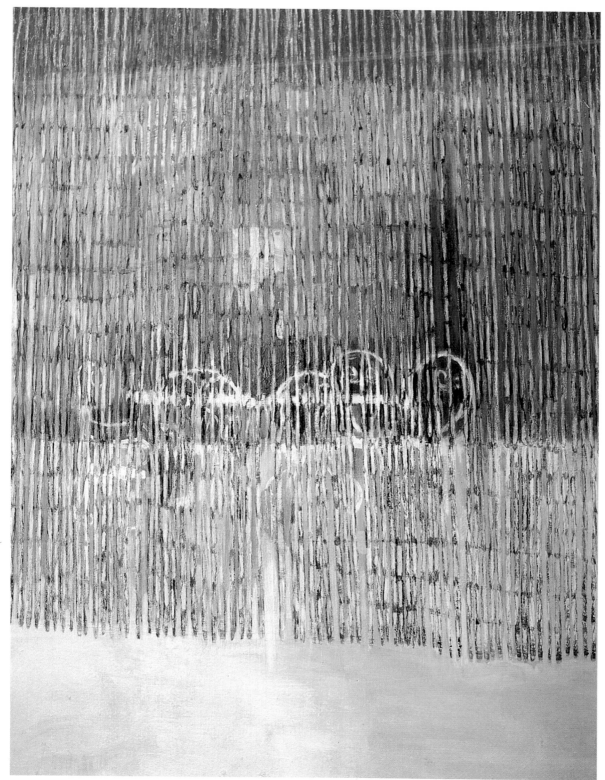

[9] *Les Rideaux* 1978

19

graph language has become the order of the day.

The "word curtain" pictures of 1978 resulted from a desire to visualize thoughts of loneliness, fear, love, pain. They were not really concerned with graffiti – nor with a desire to create literary paintings. I remember walking late at night in the winter of 1977, looking for outpourings on the hoardings and the walls in the streets of London. Why so many messages? Why do people need to see their name on a wall? Surely it's not all vandalism: I thought of these symbols as expressions of people's need for attention, as proclamations of faith and love. Surely it was the cry of the lonely? Why does a person paint on the wall of a bridge: "Pauline is our olive for ever and ever" ... and go back a few weeks later to add: "NOT ANY MORE!"?

It is from these screams that the theme of "word curtains" evolved in 1978. Images such as *Self-Portraits*, *Mimi Your Ship is Gone*, *Love*, *Confusion* – just so many shrieks of despair.

I had for some time, probably since 1975, been doing studies of "curtains on the view" when suddenly I found myself painting *Rideau sur l'Idéal* – a picture where instead of a view half hidden by the misty beaded curtain, words of love appeared. I realized then that the eye and ear should be linked on my canvas. I had found my new voice.

After a short visit to Peru in early 1979, these thoughts expanded. Here I beheld images of the myth and magic of an ancient civilization drowning under the weight of package tours. The Inca megaliths were being papered over by advertizing and Jesus had become the name of a mineral water. Pepsi-Cola had taken over the cities and the countryside, to the sound of gunfire.

The Peruvian theme played an important formative role; it matured my obsession to paint the world in which we live today. What I did not know about myself was still waiting to be discovered. My private emotional involvement was finding its way slowly onto canvas.

En 1978, la série des "rideaux de paroles" correspondait à un désir de concrétisation de mes réflexions sur la solitude, la peur, l'amour, la douleur. Leur finalité n'était ni les graffiti ni le désir de créer une oeuvre littéraire. Je me revois par une nuit d'hiver, en 1977, marchant dans les rues de Londres à la recherche des flots de paroles sur les palissades et sur les murs. Pourquoi tous ces messages? Pourquoi a-t-on besoin de voir son nom écrit sur un mur? Il y avait là autre chose que du vandalisme. Ces graffiti symbolisaient pour moi le besoin d'attention inhérent aux êtres humains, ou leurs professions de foi et d'amour. Surement, c'était le cri des esseulés? Qu'est-ce qui pousse un être à écrire sur le parapet d'un pont: "Pauline is our olive for ever and ever" ... et à venir y ajouter quelques semaines plus tard: "NOT ANY MORE!"?

C'est de ces cris qu'est sorti, en 1978, le thème des "rideaux de paroles". Self-Portraits, Mimi Your Ship is Gone, Love, Confusion *sont autant de cris de désespoir.*

Depuis quelques années déjà, sans doute depuis 1975, je faisais des études de "rideaux sur la vue" quand, tout à coup, je me suis aperçu que je peignais Rideau sur l'Idéal, *une toile dans laquelle, en place d'un paysage à moitié caché par le mouvement du rideau perlé, des mots d'amour apparurent. Je compris alors que je devais lier vue et ouïe dans ma toile. Je venais de trouver un nouveau langage.*

Après un court voyage au Pérou, au début de l'année 1979, cette ligne de pensée s'élargit. J'y avais contemplé les images du mythe et de la magie d'une ancienne civilisation qui croulait sous le poids des voyages organisés. Les mégalithes incas avaient été tapissés d'affiches publicitaires, Jésus avait donné son nom à une eau minérale et Pepsi-Cola avait envahi villes et campagnes dans une pétarade de mitraillettes.

Le thème péruvien joua un rôle primordial: il a fait murir l'obsession que j'avais déjà de peindre le monde dans lequel nous vivons aujourd'hui. Il me restait à approfondir la connaissance de mon moi intérieur. Mon champ émotif se frayait peu à peu un chemin jusqu'à la toile.

Puis, au cours de l'automne 1979, tout prit forme et je commençai à peindre la première toile des obsédés professionnels The Great Race. *Je travail-*

Cheering, Violence, Marathon und anderen lag meine Absicht darin, meine visuellen und auditiven Erfahrungen darzustellen. Wir leben *zu* und *in* einer Zeit, in der wir von allen Seiten mit Worten und Bildern bombardiert werden. Wie eine aufsteigende Flut greifen uns Lärm und Wörter an: in den Städten, bei der Arbeit und beim Spiel. Die meisten von uns leben innerhalb der Grenzen des Vokabulars unserer eigenen, privaten Welt. Die Telegrammsprache ist zur Tagesordnung geworden.

Die »Wortvorhang«–Bilder aus dem Jahr 1978 entsprangen einem Bedürfnis, die Gedanken an Einsamkeit, Furcht, Liebe und Schmerz in eine bildliche Form zu fassen. Es ging hier nicht wirklich um Graffiti – noch um das Bestreben, literarische Bilder zu malen. Ich erinnere mich an einen nächtlichen Spaziergang im Winter 1977, bei dem ich nach Mitteilungen auf Zäunen und Wänden in den Londoner Straßen Ausschau hielt. Ich sah diese Symbole als Ausdrücke des menschlichen Bedürfnisses nach Aufmerksamkeit, als Proklamationen von Glauben und Liebe. Konnte es sich hierbei um etwas anderes handeln als den Aufschrei der Einsamen? Warum malt jemand auf einen Brückenpfeiler: »Pauline is our olive for ever and ever« ..., um einige Wochen später hinzuzufügen: »NOT ANY MORE!«?

Hieraus entwickelte sich 1978 das Thema der »Wortvorhänge«, Bilder wie *Self-Portraits*, *Mimi Your Ship is Gone*, *Love*, *Confusion*. Nichts weiter als eine Reihe von Verzweiflungsschreien.

Schon einige Zeit vorher – wahrscheinlich seit 1975 – hatte ich begonnen, Studien über »Vorhänge des Blickes« zu machen, als ich mich plötzlich beim Malen von *Rideau sur l'Idéal* ertappte – einem Bild, in dem an Stelle einer halb vom verschwommenen Perlenvorhang verdeckten Aussicht Worte der Liebe auftauchten. Damals wurde mir klar, daß Auge und Ohr auf meiner Leinwand eins werden mußten. Ich hatte meine neue Stimme gefunden.

Diese Idee verfolgte mich und verstärkte sich mehr und mehr nach meiner kurzen Reise

[3] *Evening Through a Curtain* 1975–76

[4] *Dusk Through a Curtain* 1975–76

Then in the autumn of 1979, everything surfaced and I began to paint the first of the obsessed "pros": *The Great Race*. I worked on a series of large paintings which I completed later in Paris between April and September 1980. *Central Park* and the two paintings *Life in the Streets* (Morning and Evening) were inspired by the fantastic scene in New York which I had observed during a trip there in April 1980, at the peak of the Transit strike. Teeming crowds living, moving, racing, in clouds of words and noise.

Marathon and *Motion* were painted in August and September 1980. These and others on the same subject were intended to be evocations of the feeling of total human effort. They are paintings of movement, but I wanted the subjects to move within the image. I painted them in a frontal position, but when passing in front of each of these two paintings, the on-rushing men appear to

lai alors à une série de grands tableaux que je terminai plus tard entre avril et septembre 1980, à Paris. Central Park *et l'autre dyptique* Life in the Streets *(le matin et le soir) m'ont été inspirés lors d'un voyage à New York en avril 1980, au plus fort de la grève des transports publics: des foules grouillantes qui filaient à toute allure dans un nuage de mots et de bruits.*

Marathon *et* Motion *ont été peints en août et septembre 1980. Ces toiles, et d'autres sur le même thème, devaient évoquer le paroxysme de l'effort humain. Elles évoquaient le mouvement, mais je voulais que les personnages fussent eux-mêmes en mouvement dans la composition. Voilà pourquoi je les ai fait surgir de face, de manière que dans un*

durch Peru im Frühjahr 1979. Dort hatte ich Bilder vom Mythos und dem Zauber einer alten Zivilisation gesehen, die vom Gewicht der Pauschalreisen erdrückt wird. Die Megalithen der Inka waren mit Werbung vollgeklebt und Jesus war zum Namen eines Mineralwassers geworden. Pepsi-Cola hatte zum Klang von Schüssen mit Gewalt die Städte und das Land erobert.

Das peruanische Thema spielte eine wichtige formende Rolle. Es half meiner Obsession, die Welt zu malen, in der wir heute wirklich leben. Was ich von mir selbst noch nicht wußte, wartete darauf, entdeckt zu werden. Meine persönliche, emotionale Teilnahme bahnte sich langsam einen Weg auf die Leinwand.

Und im Herbst 1979 begann ich den ersten der besessenen »Profis« – *The Great Race* – zu malen. Ich arbeitete an einer Reihe von großformatigen Bildern, die ich später, zwischen April und September 1980, in Paris fertigstellte. Bei *Central Park* und *Life in the Streets* (morgens und abends) wurde ich durch die phantastische Szene angeregt, die ich im April 1980 auf dem Höhepunkt des New Yorker U-Bahnstreikes erlebte. Lebende, sich bewegende, rennende Menschenmassen in Wolken von Wörtern und Lärm.

Marathon und *Motion* wurden im August und im September 1980 fertiggestellt. Diese und darauffolgende Bilder zu diesem Thema sollten das Gefühl der totalen menschlichen Verausgabung darstellen. Es sind Bilder, die von Bewegungen handeln, und die Personen sollen sich innerhalb des Bildes bewegen. Ich malte sie frontal zum Betrachter, so daß es beim Vorbeigehen erscheint, als ob sich die dahinhastenden Menschen innerhalb eines Blickwinkels von 180° auf den Betrachter zubewegen. Diese Bilder waren ein interessantes Experiment im Bereich der visuellen Dynamik.

Mein Atelier in Paris ist ein anonymer und ruhiger Platz. Nachdem ich dort einige Monate Tag für Tag Arbeit in absoluter Stille verbracht hatte, kam ich paradoxerweise zu der Überzeugung, daß ich das malen mußte, was ich am meisten hasse und fürchte: den

[13] *Love* 1978

22

[14] *Changing Partners* 1978

23

move towards the onlooker at any angle within a range of 180°. They were for me very interesting experiments in visual dynamics.

My rented studio in Paris is an anonymous and very silent place. After a couple of months of working there, long and silent hours, paradoxically I became convinced that I had to paint that which I hate and fear most of all: crowd noise and violence. The horrific sound of men crashing into each other at an American football game. The tide of human voices coming in waves like giant flags beating in hurricane winds. A soccer game with its roaring crowds is an unbelievable experience. Motorbikes create hallucinatory messages of danger, speed, smell – always noise, fear.

The sweat of the last ounce of human effort overlaid by the storming screams of the fans. These impressions formed both the intuitive and intellectual basis of that work. I tend to work in series, because I am unable to express the whole of the emotional content in one single canvas, and I like pursuing the elusive to the end.

October to December 1980 saw me working in New York where I completed a number of paintings, but by early 1981 I felt I needed a respite from the violence. I was getting into a constantly mentally agitated state. I desperately wanted to start painting the sound of music about which I had been thinking all the while; I wanted to find out if I was able to bring together in images not directly linked with figurative reality, both the sound of the music and the sheer beauty of a great performance.

The very recent paintings of 1981, *Rehearsal*, *Concerto* and *Applause*, were about my love for the floating movement of music, my feelings for the virtuoso and his loneliness, for the moment of silence when a single cough in the audience disturbs everything. I wanted to feel and see the applause at the end of a great performance. The total concentration of invisible players immersed in their curtain of sounds like a kind of visual/aural experience in a torrent of harmony.

rayon de 180° ils aient toujours l'air de se précipiter vers ceux qui les regardent. C'était pour moi une expérience de dynamique visuelle très intéressante.

L'atelier parisien que je loue est un endroit anonyme et très calme. Et c'est là que, paradoxalement, au cours de longues heures silencieuses, je me suis rendu compte qu'il fallait que je peigne ce que je hais et ce que je crains le plus: le bruit de la foule et la violence. Le bruit abominable des joueurs de football américain qui s'entrechoquent. La marée des voix humaines qui arrivent par rafales comme de gigantesques drapeaux qui claquent dans la tempête. Le rugissement des spectateurs d'un match de football, quelle expérience extraordinaire! Les motos elles aussi engendrent une vision hallucinante: danger, vitesse, odeurs . . . et toujours le bruit et la peur.

La sueur de l'ultime effort humain mêlée à l'avalanche des cris des spectateurs. Toutes ces impressions constituent la base intuitive et intellectuelle de mon travail. J'ai tendance à peindre par séries parce que je ne peux pas exprimer dans une seule toile tout mon potentiel émotif et j'aime à poursuivre l'ineffable jusqu'au bout.

Entre octobre et décembre 1980, j'ai terminé plusieurs toiles à New York. Mais, au début de 1981, j'ai vraiment éprouvé le besoin de m'écarter de cette violence qui me mettait dans un état d'agitation mentale insoutenable. Je voulais à tout prix entreprendre un travail sur les sons musicaux qui occupaient mes pensées depuis quelque temps déjà. Je voulais voir si j'étais capable de rassembler et de concrétiser, sous forme d'images qui ne seraient pas directement liées à une réalité figurative, à la fois le son et la beauté d'une grande interprétation musicale.

Rehearsal, Concerto et Applause, *toiles de 1981, traduisent mon amour pour la musique et son perpétuel mouvement, ma fascination pour le virtuose et sa solitude, pour ces moments de silence complètement détruits par un simple toussotement du parterre.*

Je voulais ressentir et capter les applaudissements à l'issue d'une grande interprétation par ces exécutants invisibles totalement immergés dans un torrent d'harmonie: le rideau de son est l'expérience audio-visuelle par excellence.

Lärm von Menschenmassen, die Gewalt. Das erschreckende und beängstigende Geräusch aufeinanderprallender Menschen bei einem amerikanischen Footballspiel, die in Wellen hochschlagende Flut menschlicher Stimmen, knatternde Riesenfahnen im Orkan. Ein Footballspiel mit seinen brüllenden Menschenmassen ist ein unfaßliches Erlebnis, ähnlich dem Motorrad-Rennen, das halluzinationsartig mit Gefahr, Geschwindigkeit und Benzingeruch assoziiert wird, andauernder Lärm, lauernde Angst.

Der Mensch im Schweiße seiner allerletzten menschlichen Anstrengung, übermalt vom ohrenbetäubenden Gebrüll der Fans. Diese Eindrücke wurden zur Grundlage meiner Arbeiten, sowohl in intuitiver als auch in intellektueller Hinsicht. Ich arbeite meistens in Serien, da ich nicht in der Lage bin, den emotionalen Inhalt in seiner Gesamtheit auf einer einzigen Leinwand zu erfassen, und ich liebe es, dem schwer Faßbaren bis zum Ende nachzugehen.

Von Oktober bis Dezember 1980 arbeitete ich dann in New York, wo ich eine ganze Reihe von Bildern fertigstellte; aber Anfang 1981 hatte ich das Bedürfnis, vorerst das Thema »Gewalt« ruhen zu lassen, und ich geriet allmählich in einen Zustand ständiger psychischer Anspannung. Ich wollte unbedingt beginnen, die Musik zu malen, an die ich die ganze Zeit über gedacht hatte. Ich wollte herausfinden, ob ich fähig sein würde, ohne figurativ zu sein, den Klang und die Schönheit einer großartigen Darbietung von Musik im Bild darzustellen.

Die letzten im Jahre 1981 entstandenen Bilder: *Rehearsal*, *Concerto* und *Applause*, sind Ausdruck meiner Liebe zum Tonfluß der Musik, meines Gefühles für den Virtuosen in seiner Einsamkeit, für jenen Augenblick der absoluten Stille, in der schon ein einziges Husten im Publikum alles zerstört. Ich wollte die totale Konzentration unsichtbarer Musiker, verhüllt im Vorhang ihrer Töne, und den Applaus nach einer großartigen Vorstellung fühlen und sehen, ein audiovisuelles Erlebnis in einem Sturzbach von Harmonien.

[6] *Landscape Through a Curtain II* 1976–77

[7] *Landscape Through a Curtain III* 1976–77

[10] *La Patisserie* 1978

[11] *A la Recherche d'un Idéal* 1978

25

[21] *Keep Cool* 1978

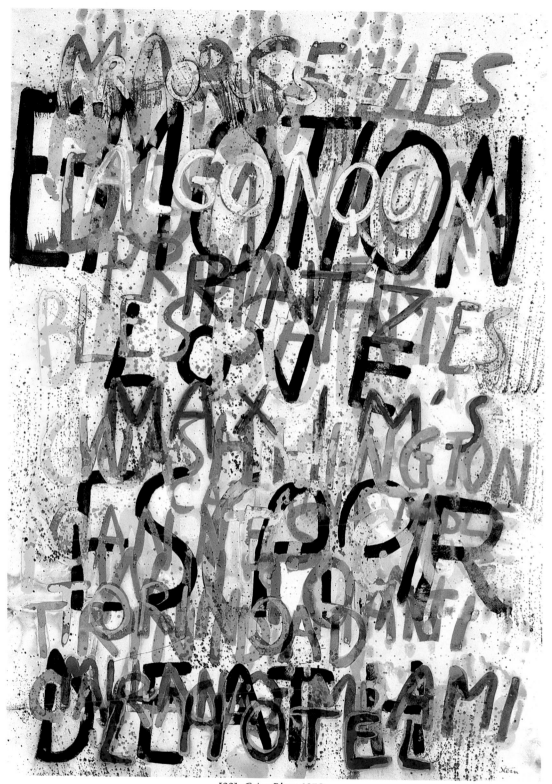

[22] *Going Places* 1978

27

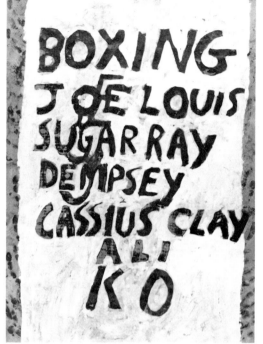

[25] *April in Paris* 1978

[26] *K.O.* 1978

[27] *Wiping Out* 1978

[28] *Proclamations* 1978

[29] *Meeting Place* 1978

[30] *Pauline is Our Olive* 1978

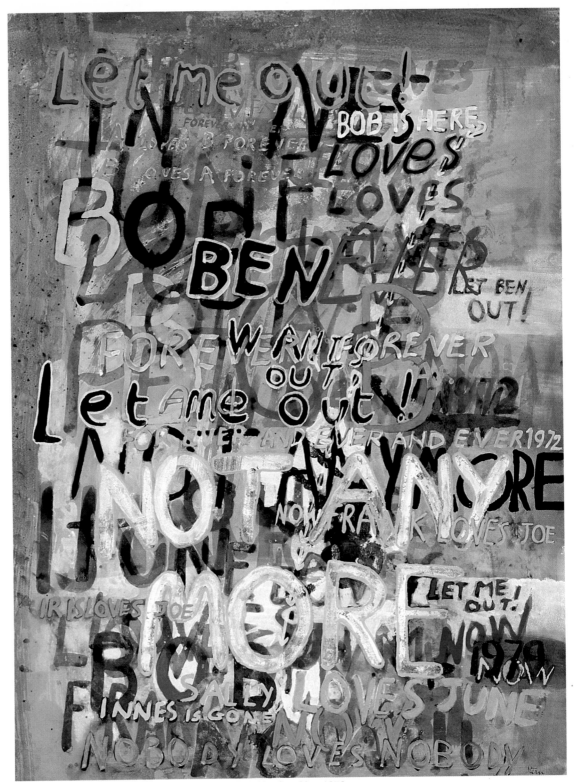

[31] *Not Any More* 1978

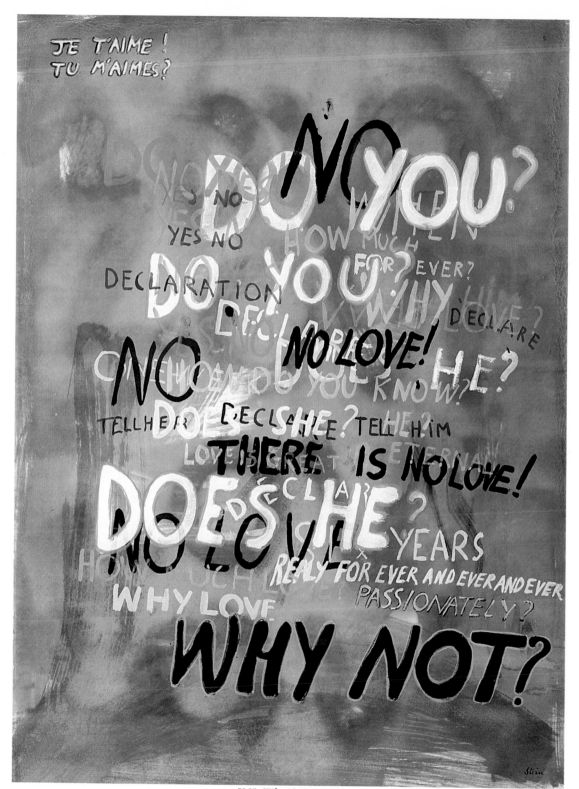

[32] *Why Not?* 1978

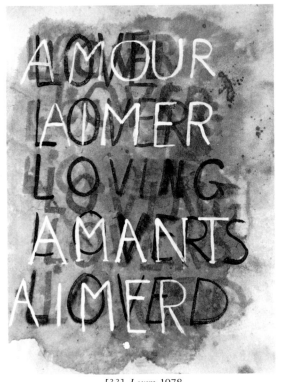

[33] *Lovers* 1978

[34] *Love Story* 1978

[35] *A Question of Religion* 1978

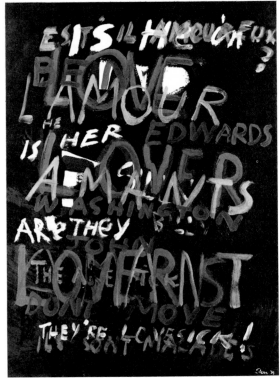

[37] *Lovesick* 1979

[36] *Mimi Your Ship is Gone* 1978

[38] *Big Cities* 1979

34

[39] *Going Places* 1979

[40] *WZ 1075* 1979

[41] *Travelling in Peru* 1979

[42] *Turismo* 1979

[43] *La Pierre Tombale de Jésus* 1979

[44] *Advertizing* 1979

[45] *Aladino I* 1979

[46] *Turismo* 1979

[47] *Advertizing II* 1979

[48] *Inka Kola* 1979

[49] *Bolivar, etc.* 1979

[50] *Holy Water* 1979

40

[51] *Go to Lima* 1979

[52] *Jesus para Salud* 1979

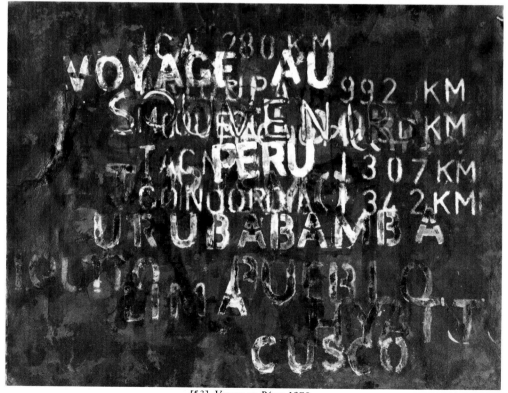

[53] *Voyage au Pérou* 1979

[54] *The Fiesta* 1979

[55] *Jesus is Better for Your Health* 1979

[56] *Mask with a Memory* 1979

[57] *Remembering* 1979

[58] *Aladino* 1979

[59] *Mochita* 1979

[60] *Hielo* 1979

[61] *A United Couple* 1979

47

[62] *Ururumba* 1979

[63] *The Chief* 1979

[64] *Battle Confusion* 1979

50

[65] *One More Time* 1979

51

[66] *The Priest* 1979

52

[67] *Volamos* 1978–79

53

[68] *Mamacoca I* 1979

54

[70] *The Family* 1979

55

[71] *Another Time* 1979

[72] *Aladino II* 1979

[73] *Volamos* 1979

[74] *A Couple* 1979

[75] *Fiesta* 1979

[76] *Ancient Times* 1979

[81] *A Soldier* 1979

[78] *Yesterday and Today* 1978–79

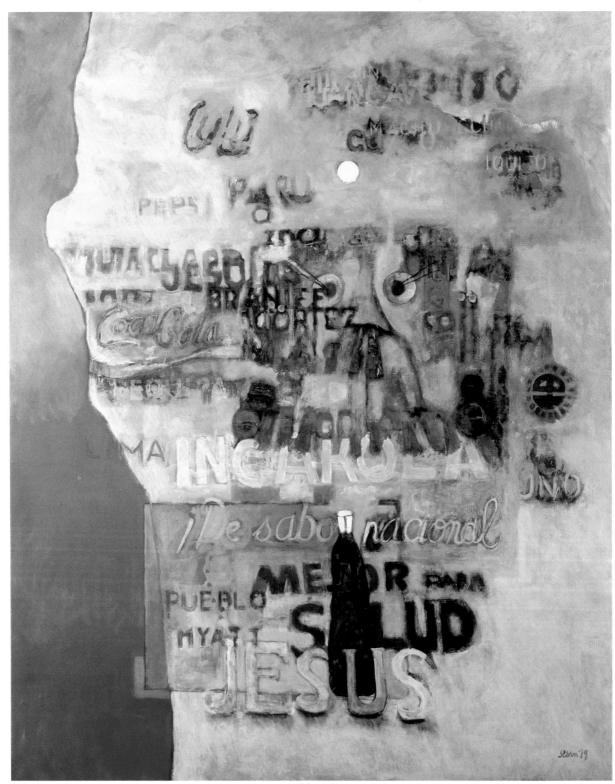

[79] *From Old to New* 1979

[80] *Volamos Condor* 1979

[85] *Macho* 1978

[88] *The Great Race II* 1978–79

[86] *Easy Rider* 1978

[87] *The Great Race I* 1978

[89] *Champion* 1979

[92] *Life in the Streets (Morning)* 1980

[90] *Central Park* 1979

[91] *Sunday in Central Park* 1979–80 →

FASTER
WOMEN
STYLE
TRIALS
SET
800 YARDS
PACE
TRAINING
TIMING
RULES
GO
JOY
CHEERING
SILVER
REYNOLD

[94] *Applause* 1980

{95} *Violence* 1980

73

[96] *Crowd Noise I* 1980

[97] *Crowd Noise II* 1980

[98] *Crowd Noise III* 1980

[99] *Fans Cheering* 1980

74

[100] *Cheering* 1980

[101] *Speedster* 1980

[102] *Fastest* 1980

76

[103] *Flying* 1980

[104] *Race* 1980

77

[106] *Team Work* 1980

[107] *Racing* 1980

[108] *Marathon* 1980

79

[109] *Money* 1980

[110] *Noise and Fumes* 1980

[111] *Fans Roaring* 1980

[112] *Bike and Dirt* 1980

[113] *45–62* 1980

[114] *Time* 1980

83

[115] *Bliss* 1980

[116] *Vroom* 1980

[118] *Speed* 1980

[120] *Go, Go, Go* 1980

[121] *Ride* 1979

[130] *Applause* 1981

Catalogue/*Catalogue*/Katalog

[15] *Don't Know* 1978   [18] *Jolies Filles* 1978   [20] *Don't Call Us* 1978   [23] *Having Fun* 1978

25   *April in Paris* 1978
Mixed media on paper/*Technique mixte sur papier*/Mischtechnik auf Papier 80 × 57.5 cm (p. 28)

26   *K.O.* 1978
Mixed media on paper/*Technique mixte sur papier*/Mischtechnik auf Papier 80 × 57.5 cm (p. 28)

27   *Wiping Out* 1978
Mixed media on paper/*Technique mixte sur papier*/Mischtechnik auf Papier 57.5 × 80 cm (p. 28)

28   *Proclamations* 1978
Mixed media on paper/*Technique mixte sur papier*/Mischtechnik auf Papier 80 × 57.5 cm (p. 29)

29   *Meeting Place* 1978
Mixed media on paper/*Technique mixte sur papier*/Mischtechnik auf Papier 80 × 57.5 cm (p. 29)

30   *Pauline is Our Olive* 1978
Mixed media on paper/*Technique mixte sur papier*/Mischtechnik auf Papier 57.5 × 80 cm (p. 29)

31   *Not Any More* 1978
Mixed media on paper/*Technique mixte sur papier*/Mischtechnik auf Papier 80 × 57.5 cm (p. 30)

32   *Why Not?* 1978
Mixed media on paper/*Technique mixte sur papier*/Mischtechnik auf Papier 80 × 57.5 cm (p. 31)

33   *Lovers* 1978
Mixed media on paper/*Technique mixte sur papier*/Mischtechnik auf Papier 60 × 45 cm (p. 32)

34   *Love Story* 1978
Mixed media on paper/*Technique mixte sur papier*/Mischtechnik auf Papier 80 × 57.5 cm (p. 32)

35   *A Question of Religion* 1978
Mixed media on velum/*Technique mixte sur vélin*/Mischtechnik auf Velin 57 × 45 cm (p. 32)

36   *Mimi Your Ship is Gone* 1978
Mixed media on paper/*Technique mixte sur papier*/Mischtechnik auf Papier 80 × 57.5 cm (p. 33)

37   *Lovesick* 1979
Mixed media on paper/*Technique mixte sur papier*/Mischtechnik auf Papier 80 × 57.5 cm (p. 32)

38   *Big Cities* 1979
Mixed media on paper/*Technique mixte sur papier*/Mischtechnik auf Papier 80 × 57.5 cm (p. 34)

39   *Going Places* 1979
Mixed media on paper/*Technique mixte sur papier*/Mischtechnik auf Papier 80 × 57.5 cm (p. 35)

40   *WZ 1075* 1979
Mixed media on paper/*Technique mixte sur papier*/Mischtechnik auf Papier 63 × 51 cm (p. 36)

41   *Travelling in Peru* 1979
Mixed media on paper/*Technique mixte sur papier*/Mischtechnik auf Papier 69 × 50 cm (p. 36)

42   *Turismo* 1979
Mixed media on paper/*Technique mixte sur papier*/Mischtechnik auf Papier 58 × 46 cm (p. 36)

43   *La Pierre Tombale de Jésus* 1979
Mixed media on paper/*Technique mixte sur papier*/Mischtechnik auf Papier 60 × 44.5 cm (p. 36)

44   *Advertizing* 1979
Mixed media on paper/*Technique mixte sur papier*/Mischtechnik auf Papier 80 × 58 cm (p. 37)

45   *Aladino I* 1979
Mixed media on paper/*Technique mixte sur papier*/Mischtechnik auf Papier 79 × 57 cm (p. 38)

[24] *Confusion* 1978   [69] *Mamacoca II* 1979   [77] *Aladino III* 1979

46   *Turismo* 1979
Mixed media on velum/*Technique mixte sur vélin*/Mischtechnik auf Velin 57 × 45 cm (p. 38)

47   *Advertizing II* 1979
Mixed media on paper/*Technique mixte sur papier*/Mischtechnik auf Papier 80 × 57.5 cm (p. 38)

48   *Inka Kola* 1979
Mixed media on paper/*Technique mixte sur papier*/Mischtechnik auf Papier 80 × 57.5 cm (p. 38)

49   *Bolivar, etc.* 1979
Mixed media on velum/*Technique mixte sur vélin*/Mischtechnik auf Velin 57 × 45 cm (p. 39)

50   *Holy Water* 1979
Mixed media on velum/*Technique mixte sur vélin*/Mischtechnik auf Velin 57 × 45 cm (p. 40)

51   *Go to Lima* 1979
Mixed media on paper/*Technique mixte sur papier*/Mischtechnik auf Papier 58 × 45 cm (p. 41)

52   *Jesus para Salud* 1979
Mixed media on paper/*Technique mixte sur papier*/Mischtechnik auf Papier 57.5 × 80 cm (p. 42)

53   *Voyage au Pérou* 1979
Mixed media on paper/*Technique mixte sur papier*/Mischtechnik auf Papier 45 × 59 cm (p. 42)

54   *The Fiesta* 1979
Mixed media on paper/*Technique mixte sur papier*/Mischtechnik auf Papier 57.5 × 80 cm (p. 43)

55   *Jesus is Better for Your Health* 1979
Mixed media on paper/*Technique mixte sur papier*/Mischtechnik auf Papier 58 × 79 cm (p. 43)

56   *Mask with a Memory* 1979
Mixed media on paper/*Technique mixte sur papier*/Mischtechnik auf Papier 60 × 45 cm (p. 44)

57   *Remembering* 1979
Mixed media on paper/*Technique mixte sur papier*/Mischtechnik auf Papier 60 × 45 cm (p. 45)

58   *Aladino* 1979
Mixed media on paper/*Technique mixte sur papier*/Mischtechnik auf Papier 45 × 60 cm (p. 46)

59   *Mochita* 1979
Mixed media on paper/*Technique mixte sur papier*/Mischtechnik auf Papier 45 × 60 cm (p. 46)

60   *Hielo* 1979
Mixed media on paper/*Technique mixte sur papier*/Mischtechnik auf Papier 57.5 × 80 cm (p. 47)

61   *A United Couple* 1979
Mixed media on paper/*Technique mixte sur papier*/Mischtechnik auf Papier 57.5 × 80 cm (p. 47)

62   *Ururumba* 1979
Mixed media on paper/*Technique mixte sur papier*/Mischtechnik auf Papier 54 × 42.5 cm (p. 48)

63   *The Chief* 1979
Mixed media on paper/*Technique mixte sur papier*/Mischtechnik auf Papier 80 × 57.5 cm (p. 49)

64   *Battle Confusion* 1979
Mixed media on paper/*Technique mixte sur papier*/Mischtechnik auf Papier 59 × 44 cm (p. 50)

65   *One More Time* 1979
Mixed media on paper/*Technique mixte sur papier*/Mischtechnik auf Papier 60 × 45 cm (p. 51)

66   *The Priest* 1979
Mixed media on paper/*Technique mixte sur papier*/Mischtechnik auf Papier 60 × 45 cm (p. 52)

[105] *Heroes* 1980

[119] *Hurrah* 1980

67   *Volamos* 1978–79
Oil on marouflaged canvas/*Huile sur toile marouflée*/Öl auf »maroufla-gierter« Leinwand 152 × 122 cm (p. 53)

68   *Mamacoca I* 1979
Mixed media on paper/*Technique mixte sur papier*/Mischtechnik auf Papier 54 × 42.5 cm (p. 54)

69   *Mamacoca II* 1979
Mixed media on paper/*Technique mixte sur papier*/Mischtechnik auf Papier 57.5 × 46 cm (p. 91)

70   *The Family* 1979
Mixed media on paper/*Technique mixte sur papier*/Mischtechnik auf Papier 80 × 57 cm (p. 55)

71   *Another Time* 1979
Mixed media on paper/*Technique mixte sur papier*/Mischtechnik auf Papier 61 × 45 cm (p. 56)

72   *Aladino II* 1979
Mixed media on paper/*Technique mixte sur papier*/Mischtechnik auf Papier 80 × 57 cm (p. 57)

73   *Volamos* 1979
Mixed media on paper/*Technique mixte sur papier*/Mischtechnik auf Papier 55 × 79 cm (p. 58)

74   *A Couple* 1979
Mixed media on paper/*Technique mixte sur papier*/Mischtechnik auf Papier 57 × 80 cm (p. 58)

75   *Fiesta* 1979
Mixed media on paper/*Technique mixte sur papier*/Mischtechnik auf Papier 58 × 80 cm (p. 59)

76   *Ancient Times* 1979
Mixed media on paper/*Technique mixte sur papier*/Mischtechnik auf Papier 56 × 79 cm (p. 59)

77   *Aladino III* 1979
Mixed media on paper/*Technique mixte sur papier*/Mischtechnik auf Papier 45 × 59 cm (p. 91)

78   *Yesterday and Today* 1978–79
Oil on marouflaged canvas/*Huile sur toile marouflée*/Öl auf »maroufla-gierter« Leinwand 152 × 122 cm (p. 61)

79   *From Old to New* 1979
Oil on marouflaged canvas/*Huile sur toile marouflée*/Öl auf »maroufla-gierter« Leinwand 152 × 122 cm (p. 62)

80   *Volamos Condor* 1979
Mixed media on paper/*Technique mixte sur papier*/Mischtechnik auf Papier 67 × 45 cm (p. 63)

81   *A Soldier* 1979
Mixed media on paper/*Technique mixte sur papier*/Mischtechnik auf Papier 58 × 46 cm (p. 60)

82   *The Leader* 1979
Mixed media on paper/*Technique mixte sur papier*/Mischtechnik auf Papier 59 × 45 cm (p. 3)

83   *Golden Idol* 1979
Ink on paper/*Encre sur papier*/Tusche auf Papier 45 × 60 cm (p. 7)

84   *Self-Portraits* 1978
Oil on canvas/*Huile sur toile*/Öl auf Leinwand 152 × 152 cm (p. 2)

85   *Macho* 1978
Acrylic on canvas/*Acrylique sur toile*/Acryl auf Leinwand 183 × 183 cm (p. 64)

86   *Easy Rider* 1978
Acrylic on canvas/*Acrylique sur toile*/Acryl auf Leinwand 183 × 183 cm (p. 66)

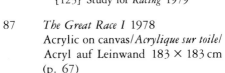
[123] Study for *Racing* 1979   [125] Study for *Easy Rider* 1979   [127] Study for *Easy Rider* 1980

87   *The Great Race I* 1978
Acrylic on canvas/*Acrylique sur toile*/
Acryl auf Leinwand 183 × 183 cm
(p. 67)

88   *The Great Race II* 1978–79
Acrylic on canvas/*Acrylique sur toile*/
Acryl auf Leinwand 183 × 183 cm
(p. 65)

89   *Champion* 1979
Acrylic on canvas/*Acrylique sur toile*/
Acryl auf Leinwand 183 × 183 cm
(p. 68)

90   *Central Park* 1979
Acrylic on canvas/*Acrylique sur toile*/
Acryl auf Leinwand 183 × 183 cm
(p. 70)

91   *Sunday in Central Park* 1979–80
Acrylic on canvas/*Acrylique sur toile*/
Acryl auf Leinwand 183 × 183 cm
(p. 71)

92   *Life in the Streets (Morning)* 1980
Acrylic on canvas/*Acrylique sur toile*/
Acryl auf Leinwand 183 × 183 cm
(p. 69)

93   *Life in the Streets (Evening)* 1980
Acrylic on canvas/*Acrylique sur toile*/
Acryl auf Leinwand 183 × 183 cm
(p. 11)

94   *Applause* 1980
Acrylic on canvas/*Acrylique sur toile*/
Acryl auf Leinwand
147.5 × 122 cm (p. 72)

95   *Violence* 1980
Acrylic on canvas/*Acrylique sur toile*/
Acryl auf Leinwand
147.5 × 122 cm (p. 73)

96   *Crowd Noise I* 1980
Acrylic on canvas/*Acrylique sur toile*/
Acryl auf Leinwand 146 × 114 cm
(p. 74)

97   *Crowd Noise II* 1980
Acrylic on canvas/*Acrylique sur toile*/
Acryl auf Leinwand 146 × 114 cm
(p. 74)

98   *Crowd Noise III* 1980
Acrylic on canvas/*Acrylique sur toile*/
Acryl auf Leinwand 146 × 114 cm
(p. 74)

99   *Fans Cheering* 1980
Acrylic on canvas/*Acrylique sur toile*/
Acryl auf Leinwand 152 × 152 cm
(p. 74)

100   *Cheering* 1980
Acrylic on canvas/*Acrylique sur toile*/
Acryl auf Leinwand
147.5 × 122 cm (p. 75)

101   *Speedster* 1980
Mixed media on paper/*Technique
mixte sur papier*/Mischtechnik auf
Papier 57.5 × 80 cm (p. 76)

102   *Fastest* 1980
Mixed media on paper/*Technique
mixte sur papier*/Mischtechnik auf
Papier 57.5 × 80 cm (p. 76)

103   *Flying* 1980
Mixed media on paper/*Technique
mixte sur papier*/Mischtechnik auf
Papier 57.5 × 80 cm (p. 77)

104   *Race* 1980
Mixed media on paper/*Technique
mixte sur papier*/Mischtechnik auf
Papier 57.5 × 80 cm (p. 77)

105   *Heroes* 1980
Mixed media on paper/*Technique
mixte sur papier*/Mischtechnik auf
Papier 57.5 × 80 cm (p. 92)

106   *Team Work* 1980
Mixed media on paper/*Technique
mixte sur papier*/Mischtechnik auf
Papier 57.5 × 80 cm (p. 78)

107   *Racing* 1980
Mixed media on paper/*Technique
mixte sur papier*/Mischtechnik auf
Papier 57.5 × 80 cm (p. 78)

108 *Marathon* 1980
Acrylic on marouflaged canvas/ *Acrylique sur toile marouflée*/ Acryl auf »marouflagierter« Leinwand 102 × 92 cm (p. 79)

109 *Money* 1980
Mixed media on velum/*Technique mixte sur vélin*/Mischtechnik auf Velin 57 × 45 cm (p. 80)

110 *Noise and Fumes* 1980
Mixed media on paper/*Technique mixte sur papier*/Mischtechnik auf Papier 57.5 × 46 cm (p. 81)

111 *Fans Roaring* 1980
Mixed media on paper/*Technique mixte sur papier*/Mischtechnik auf Papier 50 × 65 cm (p. 82)

112 *Bike and Dirt* 1980
Mixed media on paper/*Technique mixte sur papier*/Mischtechnik auf Papier 50 × 65 cm (p. 82)

113 *45–62* 1980
Mixed media on paper/*Technique mixte sur papier*/Mischtechnik auf Papier 57.5 × 80 cm (p. 83)

114 *Time* 1980
Mixed media on paper/*Technique mixte sur papier*/Mischtechnik auf Papier 57.5 × 80 cm (p. 83)

115 *Bliss* 1980
Acrylic on marouflaged canvas/ *Acrylique sur toile marouflée*/ Acryl auf »marouflagierter« Leinwand 102 × 92 cm (p. 84)

116 *Vroom* 1980
Acrylic on marouflaged canvas/ *Acrylique sur toile marouflée*/ Acryl auf »marouflagierter« Leinwand 102 × 92 cm (p. 85)

117 *Last Effort* 1980
Acrylic on marouflaged canvas/ *Acrylique sur toile marouflée*/ Acryl auf »marouflagierter« Leinwand 102 × 92 cm (p. 14)

118 *Speed* 1980
Acrylic on marouflaged canvas/ *Acrylique sur toile marouflée*/ Acryl auf »marouflagierter« Leinwand 102 × 92 cm (p. 86)

119 *Hurrah* 1980
Mixed media on paper/*Technique mixte sur papier*/Mischtechnik auf Papier 57.5 × 80 cm (p. 92)

120 *Go, Go, Go* 1980
Mixed media on paper/*Technique mixte sur papier*/Mischtechnik auf Papier 57.5 × 80 cm (p. 87)

121 *Ride* 1979
Mixed media on paper/*Technique mixte sur papier*/Mischtechnik auf Papier 45 × 60 cm (p. 87)

122 Study for *Racing* 1979
Black ink on velum/*Encre noire sur vélin*/Schwarze Tusche auf Velin 46 × 57 cm

123 Study for *Racing* 1979
Black ink on velum/*Encre noire sur vélin*/Schwarze Tusche auf Velin 46 × 57 cm (p. 93)

124 Study for *Racing* 1979
Black ink on velum/*Encre noire sur vélin*/Schwarze Tusche auf Velin 46 × 57 cm

125 Study for *Easy Rider* 1979
Black ink on velum/*Encre noire sur vélin*/Schwarze Tusche auf Velin 57 × 46 cm (p. 93)

126 Study for *Easy Rider* 1980
Black ink on velum/*Encre noire sur vélin*/Schwarze Tusche auf Velin 57 × 45 cm (p. 12)

127 Study for *Easy Rider* 1980
Black ink on velum/*Encre noire sur vélin*/Schwarze Tusche auf Velin 45 × 57 cm (p. 93)

128 *Starry Night* 1980
Mixed media on paper/*Technique mixte sur papier*/Mischtechnik auf Papier 57 × 46 cm (p. 10)

129 *Rehearsal* 1981
Acrylic on marouflaged canvas/ *Acrylique sur toile marouflée*/ Acryl auf »marouflagierter« Leinwand 102 × 92 cm (p. 15)

130 *Applause* 1981
Acrylic on marouflaged canvas/ *Acrylique sur toile marouflée*/ Acryl auf »marouflagierter« Leinwand 102 × 92 cm (p. 88)

131 *Concerto* 1981
Acrylic on marouflaged canvas/ *Acrylique sur toile marouflée*/ Acryl auf »marouflagierter« Leinwand 102 × 92 cm (p. 12)

132 *Musical City* 1981
Mixed media on paper/*Technique mixte sur papier*/Mischtechnik auf Papier 62 × 92 cm

133 *Musical Cruise* 1981
Mixed media on paper/*Technique mixte sur papier*/Mischtechnik auf Papier 65 × 92 cm

134 *Great Hits I* 1981
Mixed media on paper/*Technique mixte sur papier*/Mischtechnik auf Papier 57.5 × 45.5 cm

135 *Great Hits II* 1981
Mixed media on paper/*Technique mixte sur papier*/Mischtechnik auf Papier 57.5 × 46 cm

136 *City Life* 1981
Oil on canvas/*Huile sur toile*/Öl auf Leinwand 167 × 136 cm *Specially commissioned by* Architectural Design *magazine*

Exhibitions/*Expositions*/Ausstellungen

[16] *A Story on the Wall* 1978

[122] Study for *Racing* 1979

[124] Study for *Racing* 1979

Bibliography/*Bibliographie*/Literatur

BOOK/*LIVRE*/BUCH
Hodin, J.P. *Bernard Stern Paintings and Drawings* Three Eagles Press, London 1972

CATALOGUES/*CATALOGUES*/KATALOGE
Archer Gallery, London 6.1970 (introduction by Michael Kustow, "Bernard Stern's Circus")
The Modern Art Gallery, Jaffa, Israel 10.1973 (foreword by J.P. Hodin)
Studio Exhibition, London 1974 (introduction by J.P. Hodin, "Recent Works")
Petit Palais, Musée d'Art Moderne, Genève, Schweiz 1975 (essai de J.P. Hodin, "A Master of Transfiguration/Un Maître de la Transfiguration")
Galerie Isy Brachot, Bruxelles 11.1976 (introduction de Jean Antoine)
Tampa Bay Art Center, Florida, U.S.A. 3.1977 (introduction by the curator)
The New York Gallery Guide 5.1977 (illustration of *The Beaching of Noah's Ark*)
Galerie Isy Brachot, Bruxelles 8.1978 (essai de Jean Antoine)
National Theatre, London 9.1979 (introduction by Michael Kustow)

PERIODICALS/*REVUES*/ZEITSCHRIFTEN
Blakeston, Oswald "Bernard Stern" *Arts Review* 11.1973
Collis, Louise *Art and Artists* 11.1979
Drweska, Alicja *Tydzein Polski* 5.1972
Glander-Bandyk, Janice "Bernard Stern" *Arts Magazine* 9.1977
Kara, K. "Bernard Stern" *Revue de l'Art* 12.1976
Neuburg, Hans "Bernard Stern" *Die Tat* 6.1976
Otlet, Suzanne "Le monde de Bernard Stern" *Jalons et Actualités des Arts* 12.1976
Rouve, Pierre "Ascetic Explorer" *Arts Review* 4.1972

Rouve, Pierre "A Matter of Dignity" *Arts Review* 11.
Rouve, Pierre "Bernard Stern in Europe and at Home" *Arts Review* 9.1977
Rovera, Marina "Vivere in una Chiesa" *Vogue Italia* 6.1976
Vaizey, Marina "Bernard Stern" *Arts Review* 6.1970
Whittet, G.S. "To Recover the Innocence of our Childhood Dreams" *Art and Artists* 4.1972
Wykes-Joyce, Max *Arts Review* 9.1979

NEWSPAPERS/*JOURNAUX*/ZEITUNGEN
Sunday Express (England) 1.1966: "The Artist who Found Success"
International Herald Tribune 6.1970: Max Wykes-Joyce, "Bernard Stern Paints as a Bird Flies"
El Nacional (Venezuela) 9.1973
El Universal (Venezuela) 9.1973: "Bernard Stern, el Ingles!"
El Nacional (Venezuela) 9.1973: "Bernard Stern, Gran Valor de la Pintura"
El Universal (Venezuela) 10.1973: "Notable Pintor Ingles en Caracas"
Jewish Chronicle (England) 11.1973: Peter Stone, "A Fresh Approach"
International Herald Tribune 12.1974: review by Max Wykes-Joyce
La Dernière Heure (Bruxelles) 2.1975: "STYLE"
La Suisse 11.1975: "Un Peintre Merveilleusement Libre"
Libération-Champagne (France) 11.1975: Dr. Doan, "L'Art de Bernard Stern"
L'Est Eclair (France) 11.1975: "Un Evénement Exceptionel"
L'Est Eclair (France) 11.1975: André Beury, "Le Sympathique Bernard Stern"
Berner Zeitung (Schweiz) 5.1976: "Bernard Stern, Maler der Seele"
L'Echo de la Bourse (Bruxelles) 12.1976: critique de Stephane Rey
La Dernière Heure (Bruxelles) 12.1976: Alain Viray, "Les Natures Vivantes de Bernard Stern"
La Libre Belgique (Belgique) 12.1976: Stephane Rey, "Bernard Stern"
Tampa Times (Florida, U.S.A.) 3.1977: Robert Martin, "Bernard Stern Brushes Poetry Across his Paintings"
L'Echo de la Bourse (Bruxelles) 10.1978: critique de Stephane Rey
Le Soir Illustré (Bruxelles) 10.1978
La Dernière Heure (Bruxelles) 10.1978: Alain Viray, "Bernard Stern . . . et Solitude"
Le Soir (Bruxelles) 10.1978: Paul Caso, "Les Animaux de Bernard Stern"
International Herald Tribune 9.1979: Max Wykes-Joyce, "Bernard Stern at the National Theatre"
Daily Telegraph (England) 9.1979: Terence Mullaly, "Exhibition by Artist Bernard Stern"
Courier de l'Ouest (France) 2.1980: Joseph Fumet, "L'Univers Capricieux de l'Imaginaire"
Ouest France (France) 2.1980: Daniel Tirot, "Un grand Peintre aux Multi-visages"

FILMS/*FILMS*/FILME
Film (Colin Hart, BBC 2 England 5.1972)
Bernard Stern, Peintre Anglais (Jean Antoine, Radio Télévision Belge 2.1975 & Radio Télévision Suisse Romande 10.1975)
L'Imagination au Galop (Radio Télévision Suisse Romande 8.1976)
Nouvelles Peintures (Jean Antoine, Radio Télévision Belge 1980)